First Lady

For

Thirty Days ...

MARIKA JOHNSON

ISBN 979-8-89619-696-9

Design by Leeds Graphics.
Written by Marika Johnson

Printed in the United States of America.

TABLE OF CONTENTS

Chapter One
Marriage 1,2,3

According to Webster's Dictionary or the Bible, marriage is the state of being united as spouses in a consensual and contractual relationship recognized by law. Most women dream of being in a marriage and being a wife for the majority of their life, I was not exempt. However, the road to the altar and the union of marriage is what the two people in the relationship make it. This is my story to the altar.

I got married for the first time when I was only 22 years old, which I thought was the right thing to do because I was about to have my third child, which was his first son. I had recently given my life to Christ and still new in learning and knowing the things and ways of God and I wanted to live in the righteousness of God. So, we decided to get married. However, the next day he was gone with my ex-best friend, who was also pregnant. I had to go through coming home to find that my husband had changed my locks, and I had to find somewhere else to stay for two weeks until I could get my locks changed. He would take the car from the children and me, and I would have to walk to the store to get groceries, and afterwards, would have to take the store's shopping cart home with me. During the marriage, he had three more children, but not by me. Later on, we found out we were second cousins. It was drilled into me through the church that you have to stay and fight, and through your prayers, your husband would be saved. But nobody mentions the point at which one doesn't want salvation. Accepting Jesus is a choice and is not something you are coerced into because we cannot override a person's will. He was the sole provider, which was a way to control me. So, at one point, he left, and me and my children had nothing. I had to get the water hose from my neighbor and run it through my house just to have water. We did this back and-forth thing for ten years where he was with other women until I decided enough was enough. Oh, I must mention this decision came after I married him for the second time. Yes, you read that correctly. I married him for a second time because he came with a bible in his hand, talking right. Still, it was a deception to pull me back into a place God had delivered me from previously. Well, I will not dwell too much on this because I have some other things I want to dive into. After that marriage, I was getting healed, delivered, working on myself, and loving on my kids.

A couple of years later, I met a man of God, whom I had known for several years. We talked as friends for a few months, and after a while began dating. Then after three months of dating, we ended up getting married. We married off what others had seen in the spirit and what they thought would be a great match, but God never matched us. Sometimes it is what man puts together, and you agree with what has been spoken, and then you begin to believe this is what God is saying for your life. Then it becomes a derailment to the destiny for your life. You become stagnant and bitter because now what God put on the inside of you is drying up.

For two years, we tried to make it work for the sake of other people while we were miserable. We got to a point where we couldn't even fake it in church anymore. We were trying to hide the unhappiness, but it showed on our faces in public. I finally decided the marriage would not work, but I prayed and fasted while waiting on the timing of God. I was shocked when he got up one morning and decided to leave me, so that was my grounds to officially file for divorce. I knew he had a wife waiting for him, and I did not want to occupy a space where I had mentally checked out and hindered someone else's husband from coming forth. Knowing this revelation, it was no surprise when he ended up getting married three months after our divorce and had indeed found his rib, and I am happy for them both.

Chapter Two

The Healing Process

I have been married three times. So, let's deal with this and unpack my old traumas. I did not have a father in my life. I was molested at the age of ten and was in an abusive relationship at fourteen years old for two years. I got pregnant the first time I had intercourse at the age of fourteen but ended up losing the baby. I had a spirit of rejection from my father, and I was looking for a father in a relationship. As I just mentioned, I was in an abusive relationship at the age of fourteen, got pregnant and had a miscarriage. I still was looking for a father therefore I was in relationships after relationships. I found myself wanting to be loved so badly that I would give so much of myself too early and was left depleted every time. I learned through these bad relationships and my two marriages that the little girl in me needed to be healed. I was only defined by the words people spoke over me and I did whatever to please people in order for them to see me the way they wanted to see me. I forgot all about who God said I was in him, and when you truly know who you are nobody can tell you otherwise. Searching for a father in men was a costly price and you never truly see the danger of it until you bring your children up in your dysfunction and now, they have to pay the price for you not being healed.

So, I began to see how my brokenness broke my children and also needed to be healed and restored. I had been rejected by the ministry, prostituted for my gifts, and left for dead. God cannot heal us if we never settle and deal with our traumas. We continue to get into relationships, jumping from church to church, bed to bed, drinking liquor, doing drugs, or whatever we use as a substitute to not deal with the pain. I got myself into a deliverance ministry and became accountable to them.

We have blind spots in different areas of our lives, so having an accountability partner who can see those blind spots is so vital. With the hand of God, I allowed them to cut me open and deal with everything, even the masturbation that I wanted to hide. My body belonged to the Lord, and I was still giving myself self-gratification that could open the door to other things. When I got delivered from masturbation, the enemy came to me that night trying to bully me, saying, "Touch yourself. They won't know about that." All he could do was bully me because I had the power to decide whether I wanted to invite it back into my life.

I had to deal with rejection. I always did what everyone wanted because I did not want to be rejected by them. I had no thought of being rejected by God for doing man's will instead of what he called me to do on earth. During these years no one knew I suffered with low self-esteem regardless of how beautiful I was or if people were always telling me that. I was bullied in coming up in school and I didn't understand why and being bullied made me feel like something was always wrong with me. I was always trying to prove to others that I was worthy of their love, not understanding that Jesus had already deemed me worthy of loving and saving. I saw how many of my relationships were trauma-bonding, where our wounds attracted us to make the decision to enter into a relationship with each other. Ultimately, we didn't even have anything in common except our trauma. Our wounds needed to be soothed, and we did that when we connected.

It felt like whomever I ventured into a relationship with was my soulmate, but they were my trauma buddies. The rejection also caused me to give love to people who never reciprocated it to me. Still, they continued to receive my love, which left me drained. I was giving too much too soon and expecting it back in return. I was putting unrealistic expectations on people, and then became offended when they didn't treat me according to what I poured out to them. When I was low on fuel, I still made room to give out what I needed. I had given my heart to "men of God" who loved me privately but didn't give me public honor. In unpacking all of these things, I postured myself on the floor, cried out, purged, repented, made amends for my mistakes, and forgave myself. I was able to forgive others as well by first forgiving myself for the horrible decisions I made through the wound of pain and trauma. During this time, I knew I needed Christ, but I also needed a couch. This was very therapeutic, seeking help during my healing process. I fasted, prayed, and embraced the fact that it was okay not to be ok. I understood also how much God loved me that he would not allow me to get entangled in something that could ruin my destiny. Another thing I realized during my healing process was to believe what God shows me and stop doubting who he is in me because in doing so it will save me from a lot of heartaches.

With this new realization and forgiveness, I did not date anyone for three years. I got focused, stacked my money, and was enjoying and learning the new things about me that pain tried to keep from me.

Chapter Three

The Pursue

One of my acquaintances asked me to go to church with her because I was looking for a place to worship and be fed. The church leader gave a powerful, revelatory message and gave me a prophetic word that was right on time. While preaching, I noticed that his eyes would get stuck on me. I told myself, "This old buttercup looks great over here!" The man of God jumped into my DM (direct messages), but I told him I was still in my healing process and was not dating anyone, and he understood that. He also was not done finalizing his divorce, which had been held up in court for two years due to COVID. He would still check on me and say he was praying for me. He never gave up on me and said he would wait for me.

It was six months since our initial communication, and I decided to pray for men on my ministry page and had him as the guest. When he came on as my guest, and I saw him, it was like I had known him forever. It was almost like we were in a relationship, the way we even gazed into each other's eyes. People were viewing my ministry page even though we were in a relationship. I called him after the prayer assignment and said, "Let's get to know each other and see where this goes." He told me he was glad to finally have everything finalized with the divorce. We decided to be friends and just to get to know one another. We conversed like we had been friends for years, and we talked all day and all night. This man epitomized what my spirit and soul longed for in a relationship. The words of encouragement he spoke to me would invigorate every part of me. He felt like the safest place I had been in a long time like I could finally exhale. He pushed my children and me to ensure we reached our purpose. The way he honored me before his congregation was in such a way that you knew he had found his rib. We never officially said we were in a relationship; it just seemed like it happened over the course of a few months. I could see the weight of life and the ministry lifted off his shoulders, knowing help had shown up. This man was in love with the fact that he had someone to love his every flaw and that he had someone to cover those shameful places. He knew his secrets were safe with me, and my prayer closet would be the only place his secrets would go.

My voice to him was like the waves beating against the sand. It soothed even the slightest disturbances of his heart. When we prayed together, it was in syncopation with the Holy Spirit, downloading his thoughts and plans. We needed to navigate what God was saying concerning the relationship. I did not doubt that this was "the husband" I had prayed for at the time and that he genuinely showed up this time.

We were only two months into the relationship, saying "I love you" to each other and hinting at marriage. As I stated, I had already decided that this was my husband. I sowed 1000 dollars into him to break the poverty lingering over his life. I even got him another phone to use for ministry purposes. I was helping him in any capacity I needed to at that point. I didn't mind because this was the future; I was investing in it for us.

Chapter Four

What Do We Have?

Now that the high from being love-struck is over let us see what lies underneath what we are trying to build together. We never argued but were mature enough to have adult conversations without hurting each other. We were now about three months into the relationship, and there are some things I am noticing. Still, I have not said anything because I know it is a touchy subject. He got married at a young age and was married to his first wife for twenty-one years until her passing. They built the ministry together and had three children together. Then, some years later, he got married for a second time, but that union only lasted a few months.

One night after our date, I wanted to see where we were in the relationship and if we had any concerns. I told him that I was getting tired of him talking about his deceased wife every day and that I did not want to speak to him on the phone. I told him, "You are still putting her in your sermons on some Sundays, and it makes me feel like I would have to compete with a dead woman." He hated that I kept that from him and said he was sorry and not aware he was doing that. He told me he would not do it again. Two months passed, and we had to have this same conversation again. I'd had enough of this by now. It finally hit the roof for me when we were visiting his family and talking about having a baby. He stated, "My wife got pregnant the first night we got married." I didn't say anything, but it crushed me. The second time we were on the phone discussing our wedding, he told me that he had to tell his daughter to get out of bed with him because it felt like her mother was beside him. I thought, now this is too much for any woman to keep taking. This time, he got upset with me for mentioning his deceased wife. He told me I had to understand that she was his whole life and a big part of why he was the man he is today. I told him about the new foundation God was trying to get him to build with me and that we can't create something new using an old blueprint. It will not last. I told him I didn't have to be in the bondage of their shared memories. I told him the memories we made thus far didn't even matter because we were stuck in an old place. I told him there was still some healing that needed to take place and that the enemy was trying to suffocate the "new thing" that God was trying to do with us.

He returned after a day and said he didn't want to lose me and would get before God concerning what I had spoken to him about. I was carrying both of us in the relationship and helping him get his vision off the ground because I knew it benefited our family. It had gotten to a point where I felt like I was doing everything in the relationship. Still, I was trying to be supportive and believed the reward would be more significant. I also had concerns about his older children and grandchild, and he was trying to find a place for all of us and my three kids. I was unsure how this dynamic would work, the ground rules, and why they had been with their dad forever. I wondered how he could provide for his older daughter, grandchild, and my three smaller children. Although his two sons were working, I knew that his only income was from the church, money you cannot depend on because when people don't want to part from their money, they won't give. I also knew there were other things in my heart that I would eventually have to address.

Chapter Five

The Shakedown: Will we survive?

We went forward and set a date for the wedding, which was November 6, 2021. However, things were still happening within the relationship that I was unsure about. One day at work, I had a mental meltdown, and I called him to discuss these things and gain some aspect of clarity. To my surprise, he and his children were looking for houses and never even asked me to accompany them. I had no idea they were searching for homes on this particular day. When I spoke up about this, he told me it was not his job to ask, but for me to ask if I wanted to go with him. I told him it looked like I was intruding on him and his children and that I was fighting for a place in his life. I mentioned to him how he pursued me initially, and now that he had me, he quit doing everything he did to get me. Again, he mentioned I had to understand that he had to focus on the ministry, not just me. I also mentioned that I always give out, his hand stayed closed, and that I made all the sacrifices while he remained comfortable. By now, I had invested five thousand dollars into his business. He would not stay consistent with anything concerning our relationship. It began to clearly look as though I was wasting money and not seeing any results, not even a tiny fraction of a result. I remember saying, "If dating him was like this, what would marriage be like later?" I ended my declaration by stating that if I got into a hard place financially, he could not carry me, which was not a balanced relationship.

I always supported everything, and I fully reinforced whatever he was doing. I was a coauthor of a book he never promoted or purchased from me. Anytime I accomplished anything, he was never supportive. I was pushing his vision, and he was letting mine die. I was also beginning to feel like I was spiritually dying. In church, I never got to flourish in my gifting and calling; he only wanted me to read the scriptures. Nothing wrong with reading scripture; however, I wanted to do more and assist more in the ministry. When he worked the altar, I would have prophetic words for the people, but he would tell everyone except me to come with him to work the altar. This would be so hurtful because I wanted to be invited into his space rather than forcefully trying to do it myself.

He never asked me if there was anything that God was saying before the service was over. I would tell him in private what God would give me, and he would mention them in service, but I wanted to speak about those things God had given me. I started to feel like he didn't see me spiritually but only financially. He had no clue who he was connected to or what was inside of me. It was beginning to feel like I was coming to church with no purpose, only to bc on display as his beautiful and delicate fiancé.

I also discussed with him that I didn't think it was wise to get a house and include his children's income. The financial guidelines of buying a home needed to be based solely on what he and I could afford. After listening to me lay out all the things that bothered me, he told me he was sorry and had no clue I felt that way. He thought we were okay. He told me that he never wanted me to believe he was using me. Every dime I had given him was to help us, and he was going to start "selling plates" again and God told him he needed to stick with that and see it through. He gave his children a year to save their money and then they must find their own place to live. He told me he would start dating me again and would set aside time and clear his schedule to prioritize our date night so that nothing would interfere with that day. He also said that he needed me to stop holding things in and communicate better. To his credit, that was an issue that I had. I would often say that I was fine with or about certain things when in fact I was not. Before ending our call, he asked if I still wanted to marry him and if the wedding was still on. I said yes. He then proceeds to say that he would not let me go even if I tried to walk away.

That talk we had was refreshing and we were back on course and planning the wedding again. One morning I got up and joined in on a prayer group with a pastor and his wife, whom I am connected to in ministry. The pastor started to speak the Word of the Lord. He said, "This guy you are dating, you need to ask more questions. You have not been asking the right questions. He has some attachments he has not yet let go of, and if you marry him now, I see you being lonely. He has some things still in him that he has not dealt with. Take your time. I am not saying he is not your husband, but you need to see some more things." As you are reading this, remember these words the pastor spoke to me because apparently, I forgot them and still planned my wedding.

Chapter Six

Wedding Planning Time

The wedding date was set for November 6, 2021, and the colors were royal blue, gold, and a touch of ivory. We had a total of fourteen bridesmaids and groomsmen. I took my full paycheck that I received every other week to pay for everything. In the end, I'd put about $10,000 into the cost of preparing the wedding, including the cost of the honeymoon. He had told me he would make sure I had the perfect wedding since this was my first one, but I didn't know that meant I would be spending all of my money doing so. I let that feeling go because it was my first wedding, and I wanted it to be excellent. I bought him Gucci cufflinks as a present to exchange on our wedding day. His sisters and I went shopping for his ring, and the entire time I am saying and thinking this is really happening, I finally found love. I had an amazing bridal shower that I will never forget because my bridesmaids genuinely planned the shower for me during this time out of love. My fiancé and I only spent a little time together during this time because I worked many hours to pay for the wedding. However, I did find time to take off for the bridal shower they had planned for me. The ladies and I laughed, danced, and talked seriously about life. My heart was overwhelmed because I had not celebrated like that in a long time. After all, usually, I am the one who does things for others.

Unfortunately, he and I still needed a place to move into together. He convinced me to give him money for the deposit or "earnest money" in realtor terms that would guarantee us getting a house, but when I kept asking what was going on, he said the process was happening slower than he thought it would. He also said he needed my information to fill out an application for a house he'd found, then he came back and said his grandmother was going to fill out the application to apply for the house. The love I had for him and the investments I made in his vision had clouded my judgment about what was going on in the relationship. He assured me by the time we got back from our honeymoon, we would have a place to stay, and I would have nothing to worry about. I trusted his words even more because of who he was in God and how I saw God operate through him.

One day my spiritual daughter called me and said her friend had a word from the Lord for me. She had never seen me physically but had seen a photo of me. She was an older woman with a prophetic mantle. The older woman's word for me was… there was a darkness inside of the guy I was about to marry and that it had nothing to do with him being dark. She said there was something he had not dealt with and that I was very special to God. She said if he did not deal with those hidden things, God would make a way for me to escape because he would not let me be deceived. I called my soon-to-be husband to tell him what the woman said, and he said, "Well, I put it before the Lord in prayer." I am crying out to God like this is the second word I've received about this relationship, what do I do? By this time, I had sent out invitations and was $20,000 in the hole with this relationship. Leaving at this stage meant I would walk away with nothing because I had given all my money for a house for this relationship. Something we all do every time warfare hits is say, "oh, it's from Satan", but we forget God will interrupt our plans when it's not His will. My fiancé and I would both say that Satan is afraid of us coming together for the work we have to do in the

Kingdom, and decided we will continue praying and watch this wedding happen.

I was at work the day before the wedding when my friend who I use as a paralegal called with some news that made my heart drop. She said my fiancée's court date was scheduled for December 6, 2021, and asked if I was aware of the date. I responded to her with, "No, he hasn't told me anything about this." All while thinking to myself, 'this was something he was supposed to have taken care of a long time ago in addition to thinking about all the money I'd invested; to have to call this wedding off would be devastating. So, I called him immediately and inquired about the court date information I had just found out about, but he responded like he already knew this but was hiding it from me. He called me back hours later, saying that it was all taken care. He told me the person he spoke with stated we just simply needed to come back after the honeymoon and sign the marriage license and that it would be ready the next day since it was almost time for the office to close for the day. There was still something on the inside of me saying something was wrong, but I was saying to myself 'this man of God would not lie to me; there was just no way'. You see, I looked up to him – not just as the man I was marrying, but as my leader. But I still went forward with the wedding, feeling that he was lying to me.

Chapter Seven

It's My Wedding Day

I had to get up early and get my hair and makeup done, with the assistance of my Matron of Honor chauffeuring me around to every place. My hair color was not what I wanted, and my makeup was not the look I was going for either. I knew there was nothing I could do about it at this point, because this was my wedding day. I vividly remember receiving a call with someone asking me to stop and get a runner for the aisle. So, I asked, "Why is the bride running around getting items for her wedding?" Nevertheless, I did not let that discourage me and kept pressing throughout the day. I let one of the bridesmaids, who was a makeup artist, adjust and re-do my makeup so I wouldn't look like a drag queen going down the aisle. My best friend, who was my Maid of Honor, assisted me in getting ready for my wedding since the person who was going to help me told me she could no longer come. Finally, all the final touches were complete, and we headed to the venue. After arriving, we begin taking the pre-wedding photos and I was unsure who would walk me down the aisle even at this point, but I was prayerful. This pastor and his wife, whom I look up to as parents, showed up, and her husband agreed to walk me down the aisle. I was still sitting in the back, waiting to figure out what was happening because we were now an hour behind schedule. We took more pictures and when I looked at the time, it was another hour past the start time; a short time afterwards I was told the wedding was about to start. I was furious on the inside because our guests had now been waiting for two hours, and I loved to do things with excellence. My Matron of Honor took the wedding present I gifted to my soon-to be-husband's best man, who then tells her, "He forgot her gift, but he will make it up to her." I was crushed yet again. Internally I was saying… 'God, all that I do for this man and his family, and he forgot my gift.' I don't ask for much, but I was looking forward to seeing what he had for me. This news was another blow I pretended didn't knock the wind out of me, and I was not sure we would survive a marriage on my wedding day. I sucked those feelings up and tucked them away for a later time, and I walked down the aisle to marry this man. As he was saying his vows (which he wrote on paper), it felt so cold, and the words were so vague. The vows that I said, which were from the heart, literally shifted the room. We would have broken out in a praise dance if we had a piano player. I had people saying, "I felt chills from your vows." They were joking with him about how I made his vows look so sad and weak. The DJ they hired for our wedding was so whack that I could have just played Apple iTunes on my phone and had better entertainment.

Most people left after the wedding because they had been waiting so long for it to start. I apologized to everyone for waiting so long, but I was honored that they stayed. We were winding down and trying to bring everything to a close when I saw a plate being passed around and people putting money in the plate. I finally asked them what they were doing. They informed me that the DJ didn't get paid, and they were taking up money to pay him. (Not to use profanity), I said, "Jesus Christ!" because this was embarrassing and ghetto. Honestly, after what I had spent on the whole wedding, I was not giving anything else to anybody. They gave the DJ what had been collected and told him they would pay him the remaining balance the following week. When I thought it couldn't get any worse, the coordinator pulled me to the side to tell me we needed another five hundred dollars. She had taken the money I had for the building and bought other things for the wedding, so now I owed money. I am lifeless and numb at this point; there are no words to express how I was feeling on my freaking wedding day. I had to give them a postdated check to cover what I owed. Then it ended up being even more money because people were buying drinks from us, and that was not what I said if the bar was open. After all of this he and I were finally off to our hotel until it was time for us to leave for our honeymoon. By now, I am so exhausted and drained that I didn't have the energy to lift one leg to give him any sex. But I knew I had to because we both did the right thing according to the Word and waited. We woke up the following day, preparing for our honeymoon in the mountains.

Chapter Eight

Honeymoon

We made it to the mountains, and what was supposed to be a time of loving and learning with and about each other turned into a time of mourning for me. He woke up every morning and prayed. I asked him once if I could pray with him, and that was the last time doing so during those six days. It felt like there was resistance for some reason. I desired to be invited into that space with him and communion with God. We would be sitting on separate sofas watching TV, and he would be on his phone, and he would say he was taking care of business. He had to talk to his children and grandchild, so I asked myself, "Is this what people do on their honeymoon?" We never cuddled in bed or anything. I finally said to him, "I was thinking we were going to bond with each other and learn from each other because this is our first time being alone for this extensive amount of time." He told me I was not opening up, and I said, "I can't open up to a man that is physically here but not mentally here." He was the one who always left to get us something to eat or run all the errands, it would be during this time he was out that I would go into the closet and cry. It felt like I was in mourning. My soul was crying out that this was not what I signed up for, and I was already feeling lonely. There was a coldness in him that I cannot give language to, still to this day. It was becoming more evident that I showed up when he was in a dark place and helped him financially, but underneath it all, there was no love there for me. We went to dinner one day, and he told me that his ex-wife was sending messages, and I responded, "For what? Because you all are not married..." he answered and said, "Oh, she was trying to stir up some mess." I told him it didn't matter because we were together now.

Our trip was over the next day, and we did not fulfill what I had hoped to. I was so miserable and ready to get home to my children. I woke up the following day to the reality that the house he said we would have, in fact did not exist. There was no "together" home. The fact that we were going back to separate places was just mind blowing. I dropped him off at his residence with all our gift cards. He asked whether I wanted to take them. I told him no and that we could use them later.

Besides, I had received a lot of gift cards from my family and friends which still had money left on them. In the end, he took the gift cards. He then turned to me and said, "I will call you later because I am going to a service tonight," which I didn't know anything about. I never heard anything from him until the next day. I thought to myself that this was not how my last time being married was supposed to feel.

Chapter Nine

What's Hidden Shall be Revealed

One afternoon during the same week as our wedding, he tells me his ex-wife is fighting the divorce and that she is going against everything they agreed to. I said, "But you said the divorce was final, and we only had to sign the marriage license when we returned from the honeymoon". He turned to me and said, "She has messed everything up, and I am nervous because it means I was still married when I married you. I will let you know the court date they gave us as soon as I get it." After hearing this I had a talk with God and asked, "God, is this you with my exit plan right before me to get out of this mess?" The word of the Lord returned to my remembrance that the woman of God gave me through my matron of honor. I was so torn that I couldn't sleep because my mind was constantly all over the place. My husband was also out every day looking for another location to have service since something happened with the location he already had. I was getting frustrated because we were not together in the same living space. It had become obvious he was not concerned with finding a home for us as husband and wife to live, which made me even more frustrated, especially since he ensured me the money, I gave him for downpayment of a home would guarantee us a place. My family was upset because they were trying to figure out what was happening. After all, he and I were not living together. He told me that he had to have a place to have church, and I had to understand that part.

I continued to pray to get clarity because I did not understand anything at this point. He called me one day while I was at work and said, "Baby, I got a court date, and we can finally get our marriage license." He said that we had to go to court online on December 6. But why is this the same date my friend told me about a day before our wedding? I was in shock and disbelief because now I see underneath all that preaching, prophesying, and laying hands that this man is a liar. My friend married us and coincidentally, had been asking us when we would get the marriage license. To stall with answering my husband wanted me to just tell my friend he would call him. I reached out to my friend and his wife because I was about to lose my mind. I asked his wife, "Did my husband ever call your husband and tell him what's happening regarding his previous marriage?" I continued and said, "He told me that he told your husband this information and that he knew what was going on with everything." She said, "My husband did not know anything, and if he did, he would have never married the two of you." At this point, I am asking what else he had been lying to me about while we were dating. I began to realize this relationship is blowing up in my face. The man I prayed for, it seems, has deceived me. Now, I was feeling like a fool because we had not been out since returning from our honeymoon, and it was now a month later. It was to the point where I was completely drained and saying, "God, I know this is you, and you are preventing me from getting into something that could cost me so much more." I had so many back-and-forth moments with myself that I didn't know if it was God or my emotions.

We decided to go to the courthouse and obtain the marriage license. We arrived, and he asked me, "Do you have all your information that is on the sheet for requirements." I forgot about the documents required to get a marriage license, and I couldn't believe I did that. It turned out that he was missing something, too. However, in the end, we both retrieved what we needed to get the license. During this time, he was still trying to find a building for his church. By now he only had one week left in the deadline time to look for a space and on top of that he actually forgot the day we planned to go looking until I reminded him. I was done, so I sent him a text saying.... I love you dearly, but that's not enough, so I am not signing anything at the moment. I'm not happy with how everything has been. I can only imagine what it would be like later. I've cried to you and told you over and over what I need. I'm tired; you don't have it in you to give right now, and that's ok. I would be a fool to sign that marriage license with how I feel. I'm not a priority for you, and you have to fit me in when you can. I have no clue where I fit, honestly, when it comes to your life. These words are a broken record, many more that don't matter. When I say I have given you my everything harder than any other man because I told God when my last time around comes, I will go harder than I ever have. I haven't even been on a real date in a month, and in my opinion, I don't think you were prepared for me, and I don't believe you had a clue of what God was trying to give you. I refuse to go into 2022 and return to a place I fought to escape.

I am not settling because I deserve better than what you can give me. I don't want to hear excuses or you pointing the finger at me. I'm tired of talking; I'm just exhausted at this point. I have nothing else to say after this." When I texted him these words, it was now war between us… and God soon revealed more things.

Chapter Ten

It's War Time

I said so many things to him that I can't remember all of what I said because I was so fed up and sick of the bull crap. I finally made him aware of the things I had wanted to say to him. I knew that was not right, and I repented later. From then on (in his opinion), I had become the deceitful woman who came to destroy his ministry. He told me that I was selfish; that it was all about me, that he had a ministry to focus on, and that it was not just about me. I knew he had a ministry, but there had to be a balance when you have a ministry and have a family. If you give everything to ministry, what do you have to pour into your family? In the marriage and our dating relationship prior to marriage, he had me feeling bad and beating myself up, and now he is the victim. Seriously?...

I was starting to believe him because I was fighting for him. He was persistent in saying that he was done. His counselor said I needed help, and people in the ministry said I was crazy. He said he reached out to some people, and they told him that I came to destroy his ministry. He said, "I am back sick now, like I was in my last marriage, and my health is important." I told him we had not even discussed what I would do in the ministry. He told me it was my job to sit and love on his people until God gave him instructions on what I would do in the ministry. My thought was, "Wow, so you have a woman, and you don't even know what is on the inside of her and what she has to offer." That following week, he texted me and said he needed $60 to pay for his hotel to be able to go on his ministry assignment, so I sent it. Then he says that he needs money to get food for the funeral. Again, I sent it. He was calling me "baby" when we talked, so I am thinking he wants to work things out. He returned from his assignment and went back to being ugly and cold to me, as if I never existed. I asked him, could the children and I come to the church's Christmas party. He said, "No." I was a little thrown back by his response, but for some reason I decided to review my debit card activity because I remembered he had access to my card. Well, I saw that he had bought food for the party. I spoke with him again and asked why did he use my card without my permission to buy food for a Christmas party, I, nor my children were invited to or welcomed to attend? It became clear that this man was manipulative because he didn't want me but still wanted to get things from me. He said, "I will still give you your gift because I didn't get you anything for the wedding." I never got that gift he had for me for Christmas, but he got the Coach boots I sent him. I never got any gift cards that my family and friends gave us from the wedding. He never picked up my children's and his grandchild's items off layaway that I bought because, at the time, my car was inoperable. There were several items and belongings I'd left in his car and in his possession, he never returned including my children's clothes that I bought for Christmas. I asked for my wedding dress and cellphone because I was still paying the bill. He never gave me any of those things back. I even reached out to his spiritual son to help me in obtaining my items, and he said that he would make sure I got them, but I never did.

This heartbreak was a different level of pain for me. This pain was from not only the man I loved, but he was also my pastor, whom I entrusted with my soul, not just mine but my children as well. He told me that I needed to focus on my children, and he would focus on his; that was the most important thing to do. He portrayed himself as the victim, like I was the one who hurt him. He put one of his members out of the church for commenting on my social media post. He said them commenting on my post made it look as if they were for me and not for him. A few church members cut me completely off, as though I never existed, and stopped supporting me on my social media platform. The situation got so messy that I could not understand it anymore because we were both saved. Someone connected to his previous wife reached out to me in an attempt to share some not so flattering words about him and the previous marriage, but I blocked her and was advised to not listen to this person. I can only imagine what happened in his previous marriage, I knew then what I had gone through was not just me. He blocked me on social media and blocked my phone number. He also blocked my spiritual daughter, that joined the ministry too. She was so hurt because she was already fragile with scars from prior leadership. My mother calls him, and he calls out to her and tells her we were not together because I didn't have things in order from my last marriage. He told my mom that I said I didn't care for my family. I remember my mother saying to me, "That man is a liar hiding behind the pulpit. I couldn't believe what he was saying about you." I fell into depression and had suicidal thoughts because I had no money, job, or home. I felt like a failure and a stupid fool who was right back at the place where God had pulled me out of the last time. And this place was so dark that I thought it was the end.

Chapter Eleven

What's Next for Me?

While dealing with the turmoil of my marriage I had people who were extremely concerned about me at this point because I went into hiding. I was embarrassed and ashamed that I posted pictures of my wedding, which by the way, I noticed he never did; and now 30 Days later the marriage was over. I reached out to those who were concerned about me and got the help I needed because I truly needed help processing this pain. I went through deliverance again and recorded my session as a keepsake. During the session the evangelist asked me what spirit God said I still had within. I said, "Rejection." Ironically, she said that was what he gave her too. She talked to me after we were done and said, "You were healed before you got into this relationship, but he was not. You had experienced a lot of pain, but this was different because of how you looked up to him and who he was in God." She also said that he would have to apologize for what he did in order for God to take his ministry to the next place, or blood would be on his hands for leading the people in error. I felt much better after that deliverance session; finally, I could see some light. I repented and asked for forgiveness from my children and my spiritual daughter for being hurt in the process. Another step in my healing process was to stop wearing my ring and throw it away.

I called my friend and expressed to her I really had a feeling that if I took the ring to the pawn shop, they would say it was not real. She said, "If they do, please call me so I can fall out with you." I took the ring to the pawn shop, and he asked how much I wanted for the ring. I told the salesman it didn't matter; it was not about the money, I just wanted to get rid of it. And I wondered if it was real. The man said, "What? He told you that he paid good money for it." He turned around and said, "Ma'am, I am sorry, but he lied to you. It is fake, and one of the cubic zirconia has fallen out on the side." I laughed so hard with my friend on the phone while walking out the doors of the pawn shop.

I would have been crying and sad if I had found out the ring was fake when the engagement was fresh. Although, I did not cry upon learning the status of the ring, I was somewhat disappointed. I understood why he told me I could keep the ring and that he did not want it back. The disappointment was not because the ring wasn't real; it was the lying and the fact that he could not be honest. Six months later, I was a guest on a show to speak about shame and depression, which opened a door for an opportunity for me to have my own show if I wanted to. I posted a small clip of the interview on my ministry page, and one of his members after viewing it on my page, called me a liar. Then he wrote on my page saying that it would be a great book if it were true. His sister messaged me, who at this time was still communicating with me but stopped after I posted my interview. She expressed to me she stopped communicating because she said she couldn't believe I would do this and that her brother had been through enough and did not need this type of exposure from me. She asked me, "How could this happen when two people loved each other?" I told her, "I was not bashing him, and if you thought this was what I was doing, well, I am sorry. You just don't know and unfortunately can't see the truth." I informed her I wanted to help women worldwide and she of all people should understand because she too has been through similar experiences as I have.

Since making a decision to end that "so-called marriage", I have now started mentoring others, and

I also decided to return to school to finish my bachelor's in Biblical Study and Theology. This journey has taught me that pain will sit you right in the seat of your purpose.

Chapter Twelve

The Bomb Drops

My friend called me at work one day and said I have a case where I am filing a divorce, and the couple never obtained a marriage license. She said that in the state of Georgia, if you have a wedding with a witness, you are legally married even if you never obtain a marriage license. She stated, "I think you need to file for divorce." I replied by saying, "He was still married when we said, 'I do' to one another." She then said, "I don't care. You need to be compensated for all the money you lost in the relationship, and you have documentation on what you have spent." I told her that he was not worth pursuing to get my money back, especially when I had just gotten my mind and peace back. Another reason was that the person who married us was my friend, and I did not know what could possibly happen to him, so it was best to leave it alone and let God handle it.

Then, two months later, after our relationship was over, I noticed the acquaintance that brought me to the church had stopped replying to any of my texts and was acting a little weird and standoffish. I also noticed she had blocked me on social media, but at the time I did not read too much into it. At some point however, I did, and recall that a few months prior when he and I were beginning to get to know each other more seriously, she (the acquaintance) eventually left the church and went to another ministry. The reason she gave for leaving was that she had him on a recording speaking negatively about her, and she was tired of all the lies going around the church. The rumors were that she liked and wanted him, and by him giving his attention to me is what caused her to leave.

Despite the rumor mill, she and I would talk occasionally, and she even assisted with doing some things for me in ministry periodically. We were not extremely close or what you would call best friends, so her not texting did not bother me because everyone is not in a covenant relationship, and some people in your life are, in fact, seasonal. Well, I get a call from someone who says they want to give me some closure and to give me assurance that I am not crazy. This woman on the other end of the phone line informed me that she is now dating my ex, and she said, "I know the things you were saying on that show were not lies." I didn't know this person that well, remember she was just an acquaintance who'd invited me to this church; it made me feel like what she was sharing was true with her severing our relationship without any explanation. For some reason she ended up returning to my ex's church and he for some odd reason or another decided to show her a message where I said that she and I were not close like that. I never could understand why God would not allow me to get too close to her during that brief time, and now I was seeing why. I reiterated to her the matter of the fact that she and I weren't close. We have never gone out together; and we had phone conversations every blue moon with her occasionally assisting me in the ministry. But never a solid friendship, nor were we actually building one. I said, "God, thank you again for protecting me, not allowing me to sign the marriage license, and not allowing this woman to get close to me." It had become clear she was never getting to know me to be a true friend.

The Lesson I Have Learned

I've learned the worst thing you can ever do is allow people to speak over your life about what marriage or your spouse will look like as it normally comes from people you trust with your soul. I always thought that because of who I was, I would marry someone with a "title". This may not be the case for men and women of God. He can be a plumber, chef, or mechanic worker and still have God in him or her and be everything you need. Don't miss God thinking your spouse may come out of the church especially when we serve an incredible God. I believed that when you date or marry someone with the Holy Spirit residing in them that their motive is supposed to be pure but sometimes, we try to hide behind Jesus to cover up who we really are. I believe that we need to be honest with people when it comes to marriage, that it can be bloody and beautiful at the same time. That it will require you to make sacrifices in order to have a successful marriage.

Marriage will reveal to you what you thought may have been dead which can be some hidden triggers from trauma, that God needs you to deal with. If you both are willing to work and grow in God together it's a beautiful thing. I really had no clue what marriage really looked like because I never saw what the foundation of one looked like. It was always drilled in the church about women doing their jobs, taking care of their husband, praying, and interceding for the home but I really didn't hear or witness much being talked about when it came to the accountability of the husband. I didn't have any males in my life to teach or talk with me about relationships and my mom really did not discuss these types of things with me. I had pressure with my first marriage because the leaders whom his parents revered did not want us to continue in sin and bring children in this world with us not being married. My second marriage was pressure because the leaders did not want us to fall into temptation and fornicate and they felt like we would eventually. I felt like I was under pressure and if I did not marry, I would be disappointing God and disappointing the people who were encouraging me to marry. We, as leaders, have to stop the blind habit of marrying broken people who need healing and counseling and not a marriage license. Marriage is not the cure for issues, problems, lust and lack of self-control. A person's problems and emotional state is an issue for Jesus to resolve, not a spouse.

I have also learned through this process that you never tell a man entirely what you want or desire because they will try to 'be' what you are expressing instead of being authentic and genuine. I'm speaking of the men who purposely have ulterior motives of being in relationship or marriage with you. They will need more consistency because they are trying to "do" something that is not within them to do. Within my personal experience, I did not set healthy boundaries and allowed him to take more than he was giving. I should have never let anyone come into my life who wanted to kill the ministry in me while they thrived. Loving someone should not kill who you are in the process; it is not enough for the relationship to survive. I need to ensure that we both are prepared for marriage and have our priorities in order. In a relationship, you can't push a person beyond what they are willing to do themselves. In doing so, it will leave you drained. When storms come into your relationship, you can send the enemy on the run by fighting together rather than fighting each other. Never allow someone to come in and tear down what you've built when they were supposed to edify and add to what you already have. Only ask someone to do something for you that you are willing to do for yourself. When people have used you for what they want, you become expendable. There is no way a person can cultivate what is on the inside of you when they have no understanding of it. I had fallen in love with "the ministry" inside the man and with who I saw before the people, and I was blinded by that. I knew God was showing me things, but I didn't want to believe him. I didn't trust the God in me enough to know that what God showed me was what it was.

All of 2022, every word was that God is going to vindicate your name, and those that think they have gotten away with what they did have not. These are the exact words that had been echoed to me by Jesus Christ. In prayer, God told me one day that my husband's vows were vague because his well was empty for me, so he had nothing to pull from. These next words from the Lord brought so much closure to me more than anything, the Lord said to me "If you had of signed those marriage licenses, if would been a death certificate for your ministry."

When people you know love you and hear from God, don't just disregard the warning they give you. Please pray about it. Regarding relationships, sometimes we don't want to hear anything especially the not-so-good stuff, not understanding the blind spots we have in our own lives. I saw the red flags that were so clear, but I thought those were things that I could handle and that I could tackle in prayer.

This hit shifted the whole course of my life, and I had never been this focused in a long time. I decided not to get into another relationship until I finished counseling and was in a better space emotionally and mentally. God promised me in 2018 that I would not be deceived in another relationship, and He has kept his promise to me.

www.ingramcontent.com/pod-product-compliance
Lightning Source LLC
LaVergne TN
LVHW050342160826
845677LV00014B/3742

* 9 7 9 8 8 9 6 1 9 6 9 6 9 *